Overheard in a Tower Block

Cardiff Libraries
www.cardiff.gov.uk/libraries

Llyfrgelloedd Caerdydd
www.caerdydd.gov.uk/llyfrgelloedd

For P.S. who read in my room.
For M.M. who read every draft.

Acknowledgements
Prometheus Unbound – 3 was first published in *Falling Out of the Sky*,
The Emma Press, 2015
City Kids was commissioned by The Spark Arts for Children in 2016
Cross-Country School Run was commissioned by The Flipside Festival in 2016
Plant Your Heart in Me was commissioned by Bexley Council for
Lesnes Abbey Woods in 2016
The Story Builders was commissioned by Discover – Children's Story Centre
in 2015

Text copyright © Joseph Coelho 2017 except
Prometheus Unbound – 3 copyright © Joseph Coelho 2015

Illustrations copyright © Kate Milner 2017

First published in Great Britain and in the USA in 2017 by
Otter-Barry Books, Little Orchard, Burley Gate, Herefordshire, HR1 3QS
www.otterbarrybooks.com

A catalogue record for this book is available from the British Library.

ISBN 978-1-91095-958-9

Illustrated with pen and ink

Printed in Great Britain

9 8 7 6 5 4 3 2

Overheard in a Tower Block

Poems by
Joseph Coelho

Illustrations by
Kate Milner

Otter-Barry BOOKS

Contents

A Story of a Fear

A story of a fear
cloaked in a monster's scaly hide.

A fable of feelings
bottled up inside.

A parable of a princess
and the spell that she could weave.

A saga of a kingdom,
of a king who had to leave.

Binley House

TV aerials like dead branches,
satellite dishes like dead eyes,
rusted, but still they stared.
It was a zombie of a block.

The bin chute
made the mouth of the block.
Every day we fed it...

dinners left to go stone cold,
bags of clothes from missed fathers,
tissues soaked in tears.

The cold whistle of wind
from the corridors of Binley House
became the block's hiss for more.

The slam of distant doors
from the homes within Binley House
became the block's rumble of hunger.

We fed the block our lives:
the good times, the bad times,
evenings spent with friends who lived
above, below and side by side.

Gazing at stars from five storeys up,
smelling the bins from five storeys below.
Overheard arguments.
Overheard laughter.

We fed the block our lives
as it swelled
its monstrous city around us.

Child of Opposites

My father
could outrun the rain:
weaving through raindrops in rainstorms,
sliding under sheets of sleet,
ducking beneath downpours,
rain splattering around him.

His mother
feared his nerve –
remembering how her waters never broke,
how he passed from her
like a leaf
falling through thin branches.

My mother
chilled the sunniest day,
her breath frosting in plumes
on June afternoons,
snowflakes settling on her skin,
keeping their lattices into spring.

Her mother
feared her freeze –
remembering the numbness of nine months,
electric blankets and hot-water bottles
collecting in the valleys of her room.
Her window always closed.
Her room always cold.

As autumn grazed winter
wet leaves fell that
my father could not dodge.

Warm winds blew that
my mother could not cool.

They stuck in the sliver between seasons.
Him leaf-wet.
Her wind-burnt.

His mother
cried at the sight of a son
she had only seen dry.
A son who had never cried.
A son who bathed with handfuls of sand
and fistfuls of grit.
She drank the sight of him down with
a mother's envy.

Her mother
laughed at the sight of a daughter
she had only seen cold.
A daughter whose tears had crystallised.
A daughter who bathed with palmfuls of lava
and fistfuls of ash.
She picked the brittle leaves with frostbitten fingers.

I was a child of opposites:
constant sweat hydrating
constantly dry skin,
cracked, dribbling lips
struggling to form vowels
in summer thunders.
Trying to find a father
who dodged my tears.
Trying to hug a mother
through a prison of icicles.

I stayed when my mother slipped,
clung when my father drifted.

Smashing Snails in the Rain

He hops through rain, feathered
in tracksuit pants and pumps,
looking for snails to smash.

His path is soaked in screams
that no one wants to hear.
Beneath his sole they're crushed.

A path, in downpours, picked
from crack to twist and squelch.

The day I strayed on his
tarnished trail, the rain stopped.

With rucksack ready to burst
and ringing-cymbal gaze,
I was the perfect prey.
He flaps my head and hoots...

"What are you
gonna do?"

My whisper-thin strength holds
until he hops away
on frustration-smeared pumps,
in rain-ruffled tracksuit pants.

As rain hums on his trail
under a cloudless sky
Mum chirps,
"You should be hard."

Dad sighs,
"I was bullied."

I hear his thud outside,
smashing snails in the rain.

Welly

I spun Welly by the tail.
Faster and faster,
fur a blur
of auburns and browns.

I spun him faster
than his little legs could go.
Faster and faster.

Faster than my little feet could manage.
I spun him faster,
wanting to lift us into the sky.

Faster. Wanting to see the world merge.
Faster. Wanting to turn the caravan park into
    watercolours.
Faster. Greens to browns.
Faster. Whites to blues.
Faster. Children to brush-strokes.

I ignored Welly's growls.
Took no notice of his eyes.
Too daubed by the swirling
to see the fast snap of the neck,
the fast flash of the teeth,
realising too late
that he did not want to be spun
faster and faster,
that he had no head for palettes.

The bite was gentle but firm.
A hard and fast glare from a teacher.
A quick lesson...

Yorkshire terriers
do not like to be spun.

Light-Bringer – Prometheus 1

The vaults of gods are hard to break into,
as thin as spider silk and treasure hooked.
It takes a light-fingered thief's wizardry,
a skill to candle-shadow-flicker-dance.
To conduct through space like star-ray light.

Prometheus, like candles gasping, flicked
as quick as fireworks, cracker-snaps and sparks,
past safes chock-a-block with Higgs Particles.
He lightning-struck past chests of knotted ideas,
his mind a plume of surging thunder-smoke.

He blazed through secret halls of locked delights:
of crystal-forest planet hearts,
of spins removed from twirling balls,
of dinosaur-extinction theories.
His mind a fizz of fired-up flare.

He reaches the deepest vault with lava doors.
He hears the song of fire hidden behind,
like Einstein nicking the atom,
like Crick and Watson poaching genes,
like Hawking pilfering space-time.

Prometheus unlocks the lava doors.
He squints at beaks of flames and feathered heat,
forgets the naked skin protecting his hands.
He reaches inside and steals a fistful of fire.

Grandfather's Seal

The red garden candle found stuck in the back yard.
A yellow melted bear, head dripped away, stuck to
    the mantlepiece.
Two pink glossy puddles found on the dressing-table
    of my mother's old room.
The green residue of tea-lights from the rim of
    the bath, their smell long faded.
An orange '50' still stuck in the uneaten cake
    in the freezer.
Five cracked purple tapers, heaped like rosary beads
    in the fuse box.
A blue pristine cube on his bedside table, my name
    printed on the side.

The colours swirl in the saucepan,
releasing charred wicks like long-held secrets.
He picks them out with huge sun-spotted hands.

His fingers come out glossy with wax,
turning opaque and hard as the air hits.
He places the peeled casts into my tiny hands.

He would have set fire to the sky for me.
So I ask...

"Why is Mum always angry with you?"

The question bubbles out of me,
sets around him before I can scoop it back.
He puffs and gutters.

My grandmother's flurry of nervous activity
serves only to fan his light out.
Wax spits from the pan.

Arms outstretched, he pours the volatile
    spectrum into a mug,
pushing the wick ripped from a newly bought
    candle
into our Frankenstein torch.

The wax sets hard in the mug.
Bottle openers, corkscrews and Bookies' pens
fail to dig it out.

He smashes the mug
on the crazed paving in the garden.
A pristine solid rainbow is released.

Reds from past summer parties.
Yellows from Father's Day gifts.
Pinks from Mummy and Daddy's princess.
Greens from a wife's bathroom escapes.
Oranges from failed family get-togethers.
Purples from days when bills were not met.
Blues from undelivered Christening gifts.

Trainers

They started that day red and shining,
thick laces woven in white rows.
They were blinding,
my foot-bound silver lining.

I didn't want them to get old,
I didn't want them to get wrecked.
They were trainers from my dad
and they were perfect.

Argument

The monster
With a roar made up of shouts.
Its jaws snap
Like slamming doors.
Its stomach rumbles
Like cars driving away.
Its scales scrape
Like boxes being packed.
Its claws clatter
Like kitchen drawers.

Learn the Basics of Electronics with the Electronic Project Lab for Kids!

50 different circuits that you can build at home

It was a black plastic box
full of holes.
It came with a bag of copper-clawed wires
to poke into the holes,
tiny gaping mouths,
to make circuits.

I was a circuit wizard,
feeling electric on my father's promise...

*"I'll give yer five pounds, mate,
for every circuit you can complete."*

I flew through the instructions,
diagrams for buzzers and lights
and alarms.

*"Make a watch for yer father...
stop him being late,"*

snaps my mother.

I settle on a rain detector
on this summer afternoon,
to warn of rolling storms.

"That would give me brain damage, mate,"

crackles my father
as I feed red, gold and green wires
into the black machine, to no effect.

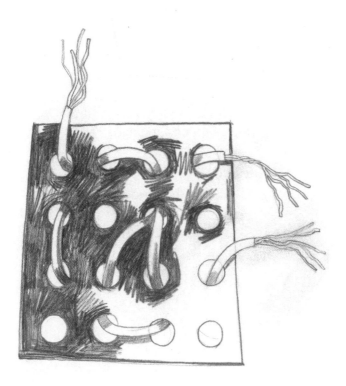

My eagle focus
turns the shock of shouts
into white noise.

There is a gap in the circuit
that I rush to fill
as they volley a battery of blame,
alternating back and forth,
repelling and attracting,
zapping and snapping.
Sparks fly.

Their poles flipped long ago.

My father charges out,
pockets filled with five-pound dreams.
My eyes cloud.
Tears conduct better than wires.
My rain detector beeps.

The Duelling Duo

In the pitch of night
two knights shared a thought,
with a sword in each hand
as they slashed and fought
on the highest ramparts
of the crumbling fort.

The duo duelled
with their dual swords
hacking left then right,
their metal ringing,
each convinced they were right.

One would hit – one would miss
in the mine-dark night
with its coal-fist mist.
One blade rang on a helmet,
hand tight on a hilt-rung sword,
both proving their mettle
in this mourning morning.

Each trying to raze
the other to the ground,
ignoring the sun's rays,
they danced their iron,
refusing to pause,
ignoring the sweat
that rained from their pores,
each desperate to reign
with their armour-bash peel.

The same thought in each head
that neither could still.
Both were right,
could not be wrong.
Apparent in their blades, raised.
Transparent in their eyes, glazed.

"I AM RIGHT."

The lie they thought
as they fought
in the fort.

The Watchers

The children felt the eyes
burning down into their backs.
They turned and saw three statues
down by the crossed tracks.

Their legs were thin and sharp,
their heads were bronze blocks.
The children grasped their courage,
took aim with dirt and rocks.

Stones clanged off the metal,
mud sucked the faceless grins.
The children kept up their assault,
then heard a malefic din.

A droning from the statues,
a blade scrapes teeth in a jaw,
a sound so full of hatred that
the children dropped down to the floor.

They quivered as the snow fell
on this bone-October night.
The statues gawped, sightless,
as the moon began to bright.

The children's knees were knocking,
tears juggling from their eyes.
The statues kept up their stare,
eager for their prize.

One child ventured nearer,
though fear told her to flee.
The statues' gazes deepened,
each peered more hungrily.

She ventured a hand to feel
the bronze-black shining skin.
The statues tensed to the touch,
the girl felt her finger sting.

A smudge of red barely visible
amongst the metal and the mud.
The children fled, screaming,
the girl sucked at the blood.

The statues on the crossed tracks
had hoped the children would linger.
They rippled as they savoured
the taste of that girl's finger.

The statues are always watching
from the tracks upon the hill.
They sing for flesh and blood.
They're out there singing still.

Richmond Park

A park,
where trees
veiled the aerials and satellite dishes,
where the sweet scent of winter berries
disguised the stench from the bins.
Where birdsong
replaced shouts,
where marshes
replaced monsters.

I ran in my red trainers
to Richmond Park.

Trees of every shade of green.
Horse chestnut trees with conkers –
like fists
begging to be conquered,
wanting to be knocked.

Richmond Park.
Arcing canes of blackberries,
berries like black-eye clusters,
like frogspawn,
protected by inch-long thorns
promising to prick.

Richmond Park.
Deer with chestnut eyes,
their irises like black diamonds.

Richmond Park.
Danger and adventure wrapped
in its dark fronds,
and at its centre lay two deep ponds.

The Pen Ponds

The Pen Ponds
Shaped like the tips of pens.

The Pen Ponds
Streams flowed from their ends.

The Pen Ponds
Winding rivers were their mark.

The Pen Ponds
At the heart of Richmond Park.

I ran in my red trainers
to the Pen Ponds,
my feet a blur of red fire.

I found a log,
a mould-slathered, slimy old log.
I rolled it down the bank towards the pond.

A giant's leg of oak I pushed,
an elephant's trunk of timber I slid
into the water.

My log bridge to the
centre of the pond.

I stepped onto it.
One step... two steps... three steps.
The pond surrounds me...

is on all sides of me,
the watery eye of a giant
staring up at me.

The log moves,
turning under my clown-red trainers
and I have to step with it.
Going faster
and faster
and faster until...

SPLASH!

I'm in the pond,
sinking down
into a watery world.

I'm in the pond,
sinking down
through zigzagging fish.

I'm in the pond,
sinking down,
the eyes of the park
shutting tight around me.
I'm in the pond,
sinking down

to the bottom.

Hide and Seek in the woods

The forest deep did hold me tight
in rustling cloak of dappled light,
as Father searched for me.

Despite his calls for me to run
away from darkness, into sun.
The woods were family.

Tables Red, Green and Blue

Tony kicked me under the table.
Screwed up my work when Teacher turned.
Drew on my exercise book.
Stole my pencil case.

Miss said,

*"If he's harassing you
stay away from him."*

I tried to move to Red table.
They said,
"There's no room."

I tried to move to Green table.
They said,
"You'll disturb us."

I tried to move to Blue table.
They said,
"There's not enough pens."

Tony kicked me under the table.
Screwed up my work when Teacher turned.
Drew on my exercise book.
Stole my pencil case.

I placed my chair by the corner of Red table.
They spread out their arms
and so...
there was no room.

I placed my chair by the corner of Green table.
They shouted and screamed
and so...
I disturbed them.

I placed my chair by the corner of Blue table.
They hugged the pen pots to their chests
and so...
there were not enough pens.

Tony kicked me under the table.
Screwed up my work when Teacher turned.
Drew on my exercise book.
Stole my pencil case.

I threw my chair across Red table,
screamed at Green table,
drew on Blue table.

Miss said,

"You are harassing the class.
Why can't you be more like
Red table,
Green table,
Blue table?"

Hostilities Continue

I didn't want to share
I told them no
And I kept it all.

I didn't want to share
I told them no
Pushed away their hungry hands
Kicked their groaning mouths
Built a wall between us
Created myths about their monstrosity
Bought weapons to slay them
Bound my wounds in spotlights
Buried my family in glass coffins
And I kept it all.

Hands shouted away
Ears bricked
Monsters bought
Cameras capturing death
I kept it all.

Caught

Our guilty knees shake.
Footsteps down the corridor.
"But it wasn't me."

Prometheus Bound – 2

Light-fingered Prometheus, chained to rock.
His eagle-pecked liver-wound burns.
Remembering the bird's blood-slicked head
glistening in the sunset glow of its take-off.
Healing in the coolness of night
his screams go out, his thinking glows.

From his mountaintop cell the world glows.
He has seen humanity surge like lava rock,
felt the regret of stealing fire burn.
In the icy relief of eagleless nights
he has watched humanity steam ahead,
wept hot tears as atom bombs took off.

His god-bound chains cannot be taken off,
welded with a deity's glow,
strengthened with a molten thread.
A punishment engraved in rock,
relief saved purely for the nights.
The days saved purely for the stabbing beak's burn.

Prometheus has seen cities burn,
watched fire-fuelled missiles take off.
His tears have drowned the stars of night.
He has prayed for the sun's morning glow,
the return of the bird to the rock,
for screams to replace the regret in his head.

The pity-scorched eyes of the eagle's head
know how hot a wrong choice burns,
how regret is a sizzling weight of rock
that no Titan can take off.
It is hard to enflame hope from a glow
when all thinking occurs in the cold of night.

Prometheus picks his liver-scabs at night,
consumed with the boiling regret in his head,
the world charred from one small stolen glow.
The heat and light was too quick to burn,
the warmth and radiance too quickly taken off,
a hopeful Prometheus too quickly chained to rock.

A glowing god, tied to rock,
heart burning as destruction takes off,
lowers his head into the chilled night.

Disappearing Act

As things disappeared from our home
I'd ask Mum questions
that she could not answer.

I kept a list of Dad's things
before they were gone for good....

His boots no longer materialised in the hallway.
His plantain no longer amazed in the fridge.
His aftershave no longer dazzled in the bathroom.
His shirts no longer trapezed on the line.
His flowers no longer popped up on the window sills.
His photo no longer lit up the wall.

Books Have Helped Me

Books have more images between their words
than any smart phone could hold.
More flavours than a thousand jelly beans.
More lives for you to live
than any computer game.

Books have helped me.

I've read about characters
who have laughed, cried and sighed like me.

Characters who have battled
monsters larger than any I could imagine.

Characters who have travelled distances longer
than there are miles between me and the sun.

When I thumb through a book
their pages whisper to me
that I'll be all right.

The Mermaid Queen

My mother, The Mermaid Queen, wept tiny pearl tears.
For weeks, for months, she cried through the seasons.
High-tide storm-sobbing, would it last for years?
Her sadness felt endless, beyond all reason.

Mermaids cry puddles, lakes and even streams.
My mother's wailed river flooded our home.
She cried in the night, she cried in my dreams,
no comfort could reach her floating throne.

I swim in her blues with webbed feet and hands,
my mind feels sodden like earth after rain,
my feelings are scattered like windswept sands.
I wonder how long I will feel this pain.

To go feels wrong, to stay makes me feel sad.
I want to see my mum, and I want to see my dad.

Seagulls to Confetti

I threw bread like confetti
from the third-floor balcony
I was too short to peer over.

Seagulls too far from the sea
would arc, dive and scream
for the chance to catch
each stale bouquet.

Not a crumb reached the floor,
all snatched in mid-air flight.
The gulls did not land,
they passed through.
This was no place to linger.

Evenings listening to the caws in your throat,
tears glistening on the phone's cord,
rolling down the nose-dive of the flex.

Bringing you tissues
made you smile,
so I brought you a box for every sob
and collected your thanks
in *papier-mâché* handfuls.

He fed you tales of flapping birds
and unhatched chicks
as he tore your plans into confetti,
your face a mess of swooping gulls.
I fed you sheet after white sheet,
smiling, the only comfort I knew.
I smiled
as your nose reddened,
as your eyes glowed.

Why didn't you snatch tissues in mid-flight?
Why didn't you pass through?
Why did you linger so far from the sea?

Crockery

*"The Mad Woman's throwing plates from her
balcony."*

My steps slow.
I skirt the willow-crowned hill,
flanking the crashing crockery.

I dive for the forget-me-nots.
Take cover in the dumps.
Make a run for the low-lifts.

In the lift, the floors sigh by...
1st...
2nd...
3rd...

Will the lift doors open to the Mad Woman?
A teapot held high?
A salt-shaker grenade?
Side plates strapped to her sides
like rounded, ninja-throwing stars?

The lift doors scream open,
I bolt for home.
Leap cockroaches,
slide past unworn door mats,
roll into my flat,
into my mother's concerns.

"I was worried!"
slips through her porcelain lips
as she studies me with glazed eyes.
We close the door on the sounds of smashing
    crockery.
We sit in a kitchen
peered over by cups, saucers and plates.

Driving

Seeing Dad's car outside my house
makes my heart race.
I zoom up the stairs – two at a time,
into his arms.

His car is like a movie car.
A strip of red lights
scrolls across the back window
like a spaceship
when he leaves.

Dad has traffic-light smells
hanging inside his car.
I'm in a lime forest,
an apricot grove,
a cherry mist.

I watch him behind the wheel
weaving through traffic
as his stereo pumps out jams
that we sing together.

Jack-o'-Lantern

A pumpkin.
A round orange pumpkin.
Cooked by the sun,
swelled by the rain.

A pumpkin.
A round orange pumpkin.
Its sunset flesh scooped out,
two eyes and a drooling mouth cut in.

A pumpkin.
A round orange pumpkin.
Its mind aflame,
dancing eyes pouring a warning.

A pumpkin.
A withered rotted pumpkin.
Sleeping soldiers wait in sun-dried seeds
for water to swell,
their promise to protect us.

The Guy

Dad's forgotten clothes made our Guy:

scuffed work-boots with cracked leather,
black trousers for waitering with a stained
    black-lace strip,
the Hawaiian shirt, a Father's Day gift. Too big.

We try binding him with too few safety pins.
Scrunched pages of yesterday's papers
leak from his sides.

We ram them back in
with numb hands.

He is slumped in a wavering shopping trolley,
a deflating balloon for a head,
a pound-shop mask for a face.

We stuff twigs into his sleeves to make fingers
through which coppers slip as we call...

"Penny for the guy!"

The wind blows through him,
twisting his frame into something unfamiliar.

The night begotten by this Halloween is cold.
We ask the shopkeeper for two sparklers from
    the packet.

We dump him on the bonfire with the others:
stuffed, portly Frankensteins with belts,
Draculas with hats and scarves.
One has a gigantic pumpkin for a head, a cloak for
    a body!
Another has fireworks in his belly.
When the flames lick him
he explodes into pearl greens and dragon-fire reds.

Our Guy is blown from the flames.
By morning he is the only thing that remains,
blackened by the soot
from where others have burned.

Wandering

I wonder if Dad's a captain
on a world-traversing ship.
But the ocean is up-and-downy
and Dad gets really sick.

I wonder if Dad's an astronaut,
searching space for little green men.
But Dad doesn't like talking
and finds it hard to make new friends.

I wonder if Dad's a DJ,
scratching records on the dance floor.
But Dad's not very cool
and his taste in music is poor.

I wonder if Dad's a miner,
searching the depths for gold.
But caves are heat-filled places
and Dad prefers the cold.

I wonder if Dad's a dinosaur,
dressed up in the local park.
But the costume would cover his eyes
and Dad's scared of the dark.

How can I become,
not knowing what Dad has done?
Is a seed free
to decide the tree it will be?

When Your Letters Came

When your letters came...
I stuck the stamps in my scrapbook,
sent my dreams to a secret shore.

A place imagined from each tiny image:
peeled palm trees,
grand ships and heroes,
a magical land

where you sat under a sticky sky,
writing promises
in sun-faded ink.

Eastbourne

Kicking the pebbles along Eastbourne beach
as the orange-pink of sunset
plays with the ebbing tide,
my mother asks...

"What do you want to do when you're older?"

There is every colour of pebble beneath my feet,
grey lumps of flint winking their sharp, shining
    cores,
gritty ovals of sandstone pregnant with fossils,
worn amulets of glass of every sparkle.

They crunch and shift under synced steps
as we stroll, towels wrapped around sand-dusted
    bodies.
The sea sings with the pebbles,
knocking a tone from each,
forming a hushing melody.

Sunbursts dip into the wispy clouds,
bounce from the greens, blacks and purples of the
    rock pools,
shine red and gold and white from the sea.
There is every colour in the sun.

My baby sister toddles alongside my grandmother,
the years between them
like the ghosts of waves already ebbed
and the years to come
like the promise of tides,
as their silhouettes whisper in the sunshine.

"What do I want to be when I'm older?"

The question bounces around my head
like light and wind and water and time
and I smile...

"I don't know."

Splash

She wants to
weave through water
with Whale Sharks.

Whizz with fish
as they flash.

She wants to
dive into the deepest depths
and land with a great big...

SPLASH!

Teetering Towers

The children floated down from their towers
that teetered on crumbling legs.
They had heard music playing,
a tune of doleful dread.

The music lulled them to the gardens
of brown ivy and frost-cracked stone.
They pushed through the wall of evergreens
but the players were still unknown.

They followed the tune to the mansions,
hidden under mountains of dead leaves.
They crept in through the windows,
through dinner-laid halls they did weave.

The music called them to the fields
where the statues stood and gazed.
The bronze figures sang a sad tune,
the children stood awed and amazed.

They placed their hands upon the statues,
three figures warm, that should have been cold.
They sang of molten bulls
that had raged in days of old.

The figures hummed of demons
that played in the fountains at night,
they chanted of the beasts
that would battle and gore and fight.

They crooned about the fairies
that lay plotting in each wilting flower.
The children floated back to their homes
atop their teetering towers.

They dreamt as the wind swayed them
to that place hidden beneath sleep.
They remembered all that the music had taught them,
the secrets they had promised to keep.

City Kids

One little boy
is using scrambled letters
to write the architectural plans in his mind.

One little girl
is using the building blocks of her gestures
to form sentences in familiar foreign accents.

A city is its children,
with their scrambled-word-filled heads
and familiar dialects.

They notice the feather-trail
behind each beggar's footfall,
they see the wing-hidden swords.

They know the city's secrets.
They've heard the ghosts in the park,
they know the football chants.

It's the tiger-striped kids
with mud splattered on each knee
who understand the city.

Who savour each street's smell:
the sizzling sausages,
the rope-pulled chapatis.

The little ones notice
the twitch behind the curtains,
the house with the demon dog,
the flower-filled roadside.

This city birthed the children
who daily wander its streets
and see nature reflected
in the hue of their blazers.
Their teachers are princesses,
they hear the sigh of statues.

Our city children
are its eyes and ears,
its tongue and nostrils,
closer to the ground,
breathing the city,
playing on the front line.

We miss it,
we're work-rushed,
screen-buried,
ear-phone deafened.
We can't see it.

These imps guard the city,
rucksack-pack its pulse,
gasp-gather its future,
clasp its embers
in snowball-numb hands.

With their jelly-baby breath
they bellow the city's flame,
turning its cathedrals into caramel,
transforming its adults into heroes.
For them the city is glass,
see-through, fragile
and all made of the same stuff,
with a promise of a rainbow at every turn.

One little boy
writes every city street
with a looping perfect hand.

One little girl
translates every city sight
with the colours of her voice.

Electri-city

In Electri-city
the children are bright sparks,
sizzling on wires
as they zap around the park.

In Electri-city
the adults are all flat.
They mope around the plugholes
searching for battery packs.

In Electri-city
ideas flow on a circuit.
You've got to be connected
but POW! It is worth it.

In Electri-city
you can turn emotions on and off.
You might be sad one minute
but then you're laughing your head off.

Man... I Had it Made

I'm amazing
Seriously I'm really very cool
When I went to school
With the headmaster
I drafted the rules.

We studied my hair
My cares
The clothes that I wear
In athletics we worked in pairs
Leapfrogging over teachers.

I say, 'Man... I had it made.'

In assembly
All praised me
Whilst I sat serenely
Up on the stage
The deputy head
Kneeling as my page
The girls played with my hair
Putting it into braids.

I say, 'Man... I had it made.'

School holidays were had
In celebration of my greatness
When the Queen came to visit
She called me Her Liege
And we sat in the staffroom
Drinking the teachers' tea
Eating their cookies
We were hated
We ate all the sweeties
From the cupboard of things
Confiscated.

I say, 'Man... I had it made.'

In maths we learnt trigonometry
By flying fighter planes
In science we studied biology
By experimenting on living brains
Geography was graded
By air miles flown
And in technology – oh my days!
We had to design our own
Mobile phones.

Mine was blinged out
Cos I was the best
It had an interface
To help me cheat on tests
It was an I-pod-PSP-Motorola
With remote control for my dirt bike
A built-in sub-woofer
To ensure I was heard right
The camera was built-in
And came with a camera crew
And the blue-tooth headset
Was set in ear muffs
To protect me from the flu.

I say, 'Man... I had it made.'

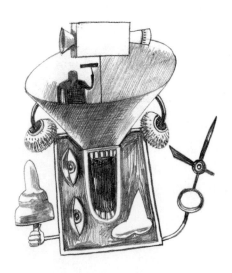

But one day I wake up
Not feeling my best
I look down and count
One... two... three.... Three!
Hairs on my chest
I call to my mum
muM... mUM... MUM!
But my voice sounds like a foghorn
I look at my nose
And it's got a pimple on!
I feel my chin
And it's feeling kinda rough!
And I keep getting emotional
About really silly stuff.

Man... I didn't have it made!

I put on my jacket
And went to first class
Avoiding the girls
Afraid they would laugh
First class was science
And everyone was silent
The topic was 'puberty'
And no one had revised it
We learnt about hormones
And things getting bigger
About personal hygiene
And BO being the trigger
Then Sir puts on a film

And there's a boy
Who looks like me
He's got a deep voice
His chin a bit stubbly

'This boy... is becoming a MAN!'

Said the teacher with a smile
Well...I took my cue
Whipped off my jacket
And the girls went wild
They took pictures of my pimples
And clippings of my chest hair
I said, 'Easy ladies, these fellers are rare.'
The other guys were jealous
But I didn't care
Because I was becoming a man

And Man... I HAD IT MADE!

Wind

I clamp my eyes against the wind
and lean into its blast.
It sucks my clothes against my skin
and blows away my past.

Prometheus Unbound – 3

Rock-rooted regret,
liver-licked,
Prometheus is found
buried in eons of eagle droppings.
Face tanned by global warming,
skin sore from acid rain,
a film of pollutants dust him.

In the setting of night
Prometheus hears
Heracles: the god-whisper, the body-thrum,
the muscle-hiss hero.

Heracles scales the mountain
wrapped in wrestled-lion fur,
hooded in tooth and claw.

Scars snake his body,
run up his neck,
frame his gold doe-eyes.
His arms pulse with the brawn of a boar,
his soiled hands have redirected rivers,
his fingers have flicked flight from feathers.

Heracles grins at Prometheus:
wild-stallion muscles twitching,
crazed-bull calves tensing,
eager for action,
giddy in the presence of this bright thief.

Heracles takes the binding chains and pulls...
snarling as his veins pop out,
twisting and surging
the god-sealed chains from the rock.

The eagle is heard before seen:
screech-wind, feather-tornado, claw-rain...

Heracles seizes its neck with one oxbow hand,
a beating wing with the other –
power floods his arms.
He pulls.
The eagle drops in two halves,
a dead feather-breath,
relieved to be rid of the taste of liver.

Prometheus hears:
the god-whisper of a city,
the electric thrum of buildings,
the digital hiss of a new world.

First Kiss

My lips
Joke-telling
Outside-shouting
Song-ruining
Sweet-savouring

Her lips
Joke-smothering
Outside-quieting
Song-making
Sweet-tasting

Bitten

My neck burns from the bite.
A hot poison skulks
thick and slow
through my veins.

My skin maps the infection
by thickening and darkening.
Boils rise and pop
into puffs of dirty grey fur.

My bones soften,
become a goo in my fur-sack skin.
New bones are cast,
forming the skeleton of something new.

Something bestial.

Bones congeal
where there were never bones.

Teeth erupt in a jaw
incapable of speech.

Hands and feet lost.
Paws with claws
wag their way into my shaggy skin.

My mind all smells,
sounds and howls.

I run.

Cross-Country School Run

The park swells its green around us.
Our youth is pressed by the sky's weight.
We decide to run together.

The park's drizzle waters our legs,
soaking our numb roots with promise.
We will run to seed together.

Dizzy with excitement and fear.
We've heard of the park's night witches
that meet at the hollow at night...
BANG!
We are the surge of spellbound children.

Threadbare red trainers press the sucking clay
as the park's air needles our lungs,
as the sky turns our skin to felt.

There are cheaters in the bushes,
preying on an easy finish,
striped with the claw medals of thorns.
We play the mile-long run for fun,
our muscles become our joypads,
we become our own avatars.
Teachers offer power-pack smiles.
As the park raises its levels
we whoop, laugh and shout together.

Our arms link over our shoulders
as the rain juggles its assault.
We're clown-clumsy in the pouring,
tumbling into the years ahead.
Holding tightrope-tight to our friendship
we finish the run together.

On Exam Results Day...

A boy's bony finger hovers
over the bloodless doorbell.

The ochre door,
opened by a man shorter than the photos
she threw away.

The boy hops forward, arms spread,
a cuckoo needing to land.
The man slinks back,
lips pulled over gums and
sulphurous cat eyes.

The man repeats the boy's name,
pulling it from memory's kaleidoscope.

The boy jitters into the flat,
chased by the primary words
mewing from the man's maw.

The boy expects to see the tawny sofa
and the osseous display shelf
that had held a plumage of pipe cleaners,
the downy ends sheafing miniature talons
that the boy had woven into a tree.

The man tries to mix
the memory of a ten-year-old
to this fluttering teenager.

An obsidian sofa,
a pellucid glass table,
a tin junior Judo medal,
where the twisted tree should be.

The man coughs up umber mutton
and quartz rum,
needing to fatten the boy
with pigments the man can stomach.

The boy sits,
all bleeding ticks and scabbed crosses,
belly like mixed plasticine.

English – **D**

Drama – **A**

Chemistry – **D**

Leaving the Nest

When I turned Fresher
your thunder-clouded eyes rained
to see your son leave.

Squinting, I leapt from the nest,
unsure of where I would land.

Egg-shell wrapped my world
and rolled through London traffic,
felt my feathers lift.

Flying in falls and tumbles
I yearned to live on the wing,

swallowing debt-grubs,
hoping my flight wings would grow.
They made me heavy.

Migrating through part-time jobs
to feed the grubs that fed me.

I dove into books,
soared through essays and exams,
built muscles for my feathers.

This Is Your Um...

"This is your um..."
rings out of your mouth
as I listen to your voicemail.

You spent decades
working for phone companies,
saving their networks
whilst yours tangled into knots
you had to cut.

"This is your um..."
Your voicemail sweats.
You stutter on the word
that is yours alone.

"This is your um..."
The word lost in transmission.

I play the saved voicemail...

                           one more time...

catch myself whispering
(so only I can hear),

**"Dad....
This is your dad."**

Plant Your Heart in Me

Whisper you love me under this tree,
where mulberry tenderness stains our lips.
Plant your heart in me.

Our young love bloomed in degrees,
my study was, by you, eclipsed.
Whisper you love me under this tree.

Others fear love, they turn and flee
your smile, I vow to worship.
Plant your heart in me.

Timeless we'll walk by the Eocene sea,
placeless we'll wander through the rainforest drip.
Whisper you love me under this tree.

My fossil love is guaranteed.
In abbey stone I'll etch this script.
Plant your heart in me.

To drink the hottest tea
you must pout your lips to sip.
Whisper you love me under this tree.
Plant your heart in me.

I Am a Father

A father
who more than anything wants to be
with his daughter.

A father
whose heart thumps solely for his
daughter.

A father
who can't always be with his
daughter.

Leap the Fence

All summer afternoon
with orange rays blinding them
children try to leap the divide.

In the shadow of the towering
run-ups are taken on mud-blurred grass
towards the sucking grate.

Strides long enough
to split a child in two
lack the wind to carry.

With punched-out stares they watch:
the hands on the scabbed knees,
the press-depress of the chests,
the pause and fire into flights.

The images reel,
feet clipping hurdle tops,
shots of broken noses,
friezes of twisted bones,
flashes of *papier-mâché* woes.

Occasional hops
kiss the boundary with tiptoes
before landing back
at the side of bedazzled jumps.

Years later,
a mid-life man
drives to the fence,
his life captured in the trunk,
his eyes poured out,
feet needing to bound.

Sodden and hunched,
moping through the overgrown grass,
clearing a run with size twelve red trainers.
The dew-soaked turn-ups
blossoming to the grey
of slightest exposure.

He places ring-shadowed fingers on his knees,
inflates and deflates his chest,
blows out his cheeks,
wipes his shirt-cuffs across his nose

and runs.

The Story Builders

It starts with the reading
of wordless titles,
with the unfolding of gasps
from pageless books,
with landscapes tumbling
from mouths and into minds
like cake crumbs from birthday tables.

Characters are moulded
as the faces of the Story Builders
squish and squash
like plasticine.
Noses meet chins to form witches.
Eyes bulge into ogres.
Mouths pout into princesses.
Muscles flex into princes.

A drama finds its sounds
as parents laugh,
children titter,
as grandparents whoop
and siblings bicker.

A fairy tale flickers into fantastic life
as silence is wrung from a crowd.
A romance swoons
as a sigh is wrestled from an audience.
A horror lurches forward
as a class is beckoned to lean in.

Here the stories are heard
between the smiles and claps.
Here the tales are played out
in the emptiness spanning stage and seat.
Here worlds are wrought.
Here stories are gifts.

A Book for a Daughter

The spine suggests a mystery.
The cover hints at shocks.
The blurb talks of fancies,
dangers and delights.

I open to a... *Pop!*

The contents are intriguing,
filled with fist, fury and fang.
I'm a little scared to open it.

It explodes to a... *Bang!*

The index is bursting with words
so precious they're wanted by thieves.
For my daughter I'm exploring this library,
I'm thumbing a path through its leaves!

The spine suggests an adventure.
The cover hides a tomb.
The blurb talks of mummies,
ghosts and ghouls.

I open to a... *Boom!*

The contents are intriguing,
things that I have never said.
She'll open this book and find
she's always in my head.

The index is heaving with words,
shouted words,
words I wish
to rain on her from above.

She'll open this book and find
it's filled with a father's love.

There are Things that Lurk in the Library

There are things that lurk in the library,
that thumb and squeeze between the leaves.
New worlds can be found in the books,
characters listen to all that you read.
There are whisperings between the words
and shivers rearing to leap on your spine.

Run your fingertips along the spine,
feel the bones of each book in your library.
Watch amazed as the muscle-words
flex! Robbed of the will to leave,
you are compelled to stay and read.
There are worlds to be found in these books.

There are worlds to be found in these books:
ideas that wise minds have opined,
tales of the deepest red.
Unknown narratives skulk in this library
where parables rustle like leaves,
where mouths taste new words.

There are sagas in you if you look inward.
Your whole life could be read as a book,
all your fears bound into uncut leaves.
Fairy tales are written on your spine.
Every wrinkle has its own library,
every crease is waiting to be read.

We leave volumes wherever we tread.
Every sigh has its own hidden word,
every hug is its own library,
every goodbye a dog-eared book,
every choice bound to a moral spine,
a story we can never leave.

As your book forms its leaves,
as you leave a story for others to read,
make sure you bind well your spine.
Don't let the ink smudge on a word.

For you yourself are a book.
You yourself are a library.

JOSEPH COELHO's debut children's poetry collection, *Werewolf Club Rules*, was the winner of the CLiPPA Award in 2015. His poems have also been published in several anthologies including *Green Glass Beads*, edited by Jacqueline Wilson. Joseph has been a guest poet on Cbeebies Rhyme Rocket and has worked alongside Valerie Bloom and Michael Rosen for CBeebies Radio on Poetry Playtime. He has written plays for companies including The Unicorn Theatre, Polka Theatre, Theatre Royal York, and The Spark Children's Festival and performed his solo shows up and down the country in association with Half Moon Theatre. His plays have received special note from the Verity Bargate Award and The Bruntwood Playwriting Competition. He lives in Kent.

KATE MILNER studied Illustration at Central St Martin's before completing an MA in Children's Book Illustration at Anglia Ruskin University. Her work has been published in magazines and her illustrations and prints have been shown in London galleries and national touring exhibitions. Kate won the V&A Student Illustration Award in 2016. She is the author and illustrator of *My Name is not Refugee*, published in 2017. She lives in Leighton Buzzard, Bedfordshire.